CHOOSE

Steer Wide of Total Stupidity

Kevin Johnson

CHOOSE

Steer Wide of Total Stupidity

Kevin Johnson

DEEPER SERIES

ZONDERVAN®

ZONDERVAN.com/
AUTHORTRACKER
follow your favorite authors

**youth
specialties**

**youth
specialties**

Choose: Steer Wide of Total Stupidity
Copyright 2007 by Kevin Johnson

Youth Specialties resources, 300 S. Pierce St., El Cajon, CA 92020 are published by
Zondervan, 5300 Patterson Ave. SE, Grand Rapids, MI 49530.

Library of Congress Cataloging-in-Publication Data

Johnson, Kevin (Kevin Walter)
  Choose : steer wide of total stupidity / By Kevin Johnson.
    p. cm.
  ISBN-10: 0-310-27493-1 (pbk.)
  ISBN-13: 978-0-310-27493-3 (pbk.)
  1. Christian life—Biblical teaching—Juvenile literature. 2. Junior high
school students—Conduct of life—Juvenile literature. I. Title.
  BS680.C47J625 2007
  248.8'3—dc22

                                                                    2007039357

Cover and interior design by SharpSeven Design

Printed in the United States of America

---

10 11 12 • 20 19 18 17 16 15 14 13 12 11 10 9 8 7 6

Contents

Start Here

It's cool that you're cracking open this book. If you've ever wanted to dig into the Bible or find out what it takes to grow in your faith, the DEEPER series is like an enormous neon finger that'll point you toward exactly what you need to know.

Choose contains 20 Bible studies that build piece by piece. You'll check out Scripture, think for yourself, and feed on insights you might not otherwise find. This book points you toward God's smart way to do life and helps you meet your most baffling challenges head on. You'll discover that making amazingly good choices isn't meant to ruin your day. It's how you experience total closeness to God and avoid hitting the big fan of life. After all, God is the One who made you. He knows the wisest ways to get through life. And he doesn't want you to settle for anything less than his best.

Don't rush through the book. Pick your own pace—from a study per day to a study per week. Actually, the slower you go, the more you'll gain. While each study is just a couple of pages long, every one of them is tagged with another page of bonus material that can help you dig even deeper.

Each study opens with a mostly blank page that has a single Bible verse that sums up the main point. These verses are worth memorizing, as a way to lock your head on to the awesome truths of God's Word. Then comes **START**, a brief intro to get your brain geared up for the topic. **READ** takes you to a short Scripture passage. You can read it here in the book or, if you want, grab your own Bible and read the passage there. **THINK** helps you examine the main ideas of the passage, and **LIVE** makes it easy to apply what you learn. **WRAP** pulls everything together.

Then there's that bonus material. **MORE THOUGHTS TO MULL** tosses you a few more questions to ask yourself or others. **MORE SCRIPTURES TO DIG** leads you to related Bible passages to get you the full scoop on a topic.

Whether you read on your own or get together with a group, *Choose* will help you take your next step in becoming wildly devoted to Jesus. If you're ready to grab hold of a heart-to-heart, all-out relationship with God, dig in!

1. THE BODY-SIZED BLENDER

Wanting God's wisdom

Proverbs 2:6

For the Lord gives wisdom;

from his mouth come knowledge and understanding.

➔   **START** You scramble over a barbed-wire fence emblazoned with a giant KEEP OUT sign, bolt past airport security, and crawl across a runway. Then you ignore the simple yet bold warning on the side of the plane☐ a sticker that maps the zone of death in front of the jet engines, where those roaring turbines suck in anything nearby. You thought the best way to understand a jet engine would be to get an up-close look. Now you're about to get an up-close exam, all right. Like touring the inside of a body-sized blender.

How do you usually respond to rules about what you should do, or warnings and cautions telling you not to do something?

➔   **READ** Proverbs 2:1-8

¹My son, if you accept my words

and store up my commands within you,

²turning your ear to wisdom

and applying your heart to understanding—

³indeed, if you call out for insight

and cry aloud for understanding,

⁴and if you look for it as for silver

and search for it as for hidden treasure,

⁵then you will understand the fear of the Lord

and find the knowledge of God.

⁶For the Lord gives wisdom;

from his mouth come knowledge and understanding.

⁷He holds success in store for the upright,

he is a shield to those whose walk is blameless,

⁸for he guards the course of the just

and protects the way of his faithful ones.

➡ **THINK** God's wisdom is what keeps you from hitting the big fan of life. But God doesn't force you to obey. Instead, he insists on engaging your mind and your heart in making smart choices. At the start of this passage, there are several "ifs" that involve you. Find them. Circle them. (If you count all the phrases in the first four verses, then you should discover eight altogether.)

All those "ifs" sound like a lot of work. But what do you get if you search hard for wisdom? Jot down several of the payoffs listed in verses 5-8. Circle two that sound the best to you. Why do those sound so good?

under Standing
fear of the Lord
Knowlege
Wisdom
Success
Sheild or protector

"The fear of the Lord," by the way, is the healthy respect you should rightly have for God, the one true King of the universe. And the knowledge you get from God is nothing less than the jaw-dropping, awe-inspiring, life-changing insight you'd expect from the One who is not only all-powerful, but also all-knowing and all-kind. Proverbs 1:7 says, "The fear of the Lord [or "respect for the Lord"] is the beginning of knowledge, but fools despise wisdom and instruction."

➜   **LIVE** When have you been helped by a warning—from a friend, a parent, a teacher, or even a stranger?

Do you think God shares his wisdom in order to ruin your life—or to make it wildly enjoyable? Why do you think that?

How important is it to you to get God's smarts? Explain.

➜   **WRAP** The Bible is packed with wisdom that's even better than an oversized sticker that keeps you from getting sucked into a spinning turbine. It's know-how that can help you stay close to God and steer clear of the stupidity of sin. What you need from the start, however, are good reasons and a great desire to get God's help. It's how you jump into the good life he intends for you.

》 MORE THOUGHTS TO MULL

- What's the dumbest thing you've ever been spared from doing because someone got involved and pointed you to something smarter?

- Life is full of *don't-run-with-scissors* rules. What kinds of rules— maybe good, maybe pointless—drive you nuts?

- Ask an adult, "Who was the smartest person you ever knew?" Follow up with these queries: "What kind of intelligence did he or she have?" and "How did those smarts make a positive difference for that person or for others?"

》 MORE SCRIPTURES TO DIG

- Keep going and read three more verses, **Proverbs 2:9-11:** "Then you will understand what is right and just and fair—every good path. For wisdom will enter your heart, and knowledge will be pleasant to your soul. Discretion will protect you, and understanding will guard you." Honestly, how helpful do you think God's wisdom is to you? How does it lead you into "every good path"? How is it "pleasant"? How might it "protect you"?

- If you have any doubt about whether God has the best in mind for you in all that he tells you to do or not do, ponder these two Bible verses. God once spoke through the prophet Jeremiah and said, "I know the plans I have for you...plans to prosper you and not to harm you, plans to give you hope and a future" (**Jeremiah 29:11**). Jesus took the same basic idea and phrased it this way: "I have come that they may have life, and have it to the full" (**John 10:10**).

- Read **Proverbs 1** for a bunch more reasons why God's wisdom is what you want to get.

2. TOTALLY BLESSED

Good things happen when you stick to God

Psalm 1:1-2

Blessed are those who do not walk in step with the wicked

or stand in the way that sinners take

or sit in the company of mockers,

but who delight in the law of the Lord and meditate on his law day and night.

➜ **START** Think hard about the first word in this Bible passage—*blessed*—because it explains everything good that comes after it. You might think *blessed* is a word only spoken by saintly old grandmas. But in the Bible, *blessed* actually means something closer to "fortunate" or even "happy." Yet being "blessed" isn't a fleeting feeling. It's deep peace and satisfaction that comes from doing life God's way.

How could having a relationship with God leave you feeling blessed? As you think about your everyday life, what's hot about following God—and what's not?

➜ **READ** Psalm 1:1-6

¹Blessed are those who do not walk in step with the wicked or stand in the way that sinners take or sit in the company of mockers, ²but who delight in the law of the Lord and meditate on his law day and night. ³They are like a tree planted by streams of water, which yields its fruit in season and whose leaf does not wither—whatever they do prospers. ⁴Not so the wicked! They are like chaff that the wind blows away. ⁵Therefore the wicked will not stand in the judgment, nor sinners in the assembly of the righteous. ⁶For the Lord watches over the way of the righteous, but the way of the wicked will be destroyed.

➜ **THINK** Jot down five things you notice in this passage about a blessed person.

Some people see stages of badness at the start of this Psalm—like how a person first trips, then tumbles, and finally lands with a splat. To get in step with the wicked—that's bad. To side with sinners—that's deeper trouble. And to grab a seat with people who mock God—you're truly stuck in sin. If instead you learn God's ways, then you'll avoid all that.

While people who are wicked, sinful, and cynical are doing their thing, what is the person blessed by God up to?

Meditate literally means "mutter." Back in Bible times, people seldom had access to written Scripture. So they memorized passages and continually rolled them around in their heads to get full of God's wisdom.

What happens to people who choose to ponder God's words—and act on them? What happens to those who choose a different way?

This psalm wasn't written by someone sipping Slushees by a pool. It comes from the heart of arid Israel. The point? God's followers aren't like stunted trees that rely on luck for an occasional drop of rain. They're like trees planted next to a stream—or, actually, an irrigation ditch. They lap up regular, reliable refreshment that's sent from the One who planted them.

➔   **LIVE** Of all the people in your world—peers, parents, celebrities, media, teachers, siblings—who defines for you whether a choice is a smart one? How much do those "experts" agree with God's wisdom—or not?

How would your life be different right now if you stuck close to God's stream? In other words, what would change if you continually gained wisdom from God and then lived what you know as best you can?

➔   **WRAP** God wants to plant you by the stream of his life-giving wisdom and help you make life-altering choices for good. You can drink up and get wise for today and every day, but only if you want to.

» MORE THOUGHTS TO MULL

- What keeps you from giving God your wild, wholehearted obedience? What sounds unappealing about gulping from God's stream of wisdom?

- At first the blessed person in this Bible passage might sound like a solo act. But verse 5 says there's an "assembly of the righteous," a group of people who follow God. Who in your life wants to go deep with God? Do you have anyone who could study *Choose* with you?

- Some people ignore God, reject his commands, and still do great in life. How do you explain that?

» MORE SCRIPTURES TO DIG

- God doesn't guarantee an immediate payoff for making great choices. If you've ever wondered why nasty people don't immediately blow away in the breeze, look at **Psalm 73**. It offers dazzling insight into both the fate of evildoers and God's unfailing care for his people. It's a little long, but it helps make sense of some of life's toughest puzzles. And it also reminds you why hanging tight with God is the right choice.

- One of Jesus' best-known teachings loudly echoes this "blessed" theme. His Sermon on the Mount starts with the words "Blessed are the poor in spirit, for theirs is the kingdom of heaven." Read **Matthew 5:1-12** for teachings that turn the logic of our world upside down. If your Bible version uses the word *blessed*, check how the passage sounds when you swap in the word *happy* instead. Just remember that *happy* doesn't mean a frothy feeling. It's that deep peace that doesn't end.

- The apostle Paul sums up the greatest blessing anyone can ever get. Check out **Romans 4:7-8**: "Oh, what joy for those whose disobedience is forgiven, whose sins are put out of sight. Yes, what joy for those whose record the Lord has cleared of sin" (NLT).

3. GOT BRAINS?

God's flawless wisdom

Psalm 19:7

The law of the Lord is perfect, refreshing the soul.

➔   **START** When you go fishing in unfamiliar waters, it's smart to hire a guide. If you want to hunt down the homes of Hollywood stars, you should start with a map. If you hope to assemble some complicated thingy, it pays to read the directions. But like every kind of information in life, those instructions are only as good as their source. Before you let anyone tell you how to live, you'd better make sure they're right.

Whom do you count on the most to help you choose the best path for your life? Share why that person is tops.

➔   **READ** Psalm 19:7-11

⁷The law of the Lord is perfect, refreshing the soul.

The statutes of the Lord are trustworthy, making wise the simple.

⁸The precepts of the Lord are right, giving joy to the heart.

The commands of the Lord are radiant, giving light to the eyes.

⁹The fear of the Lord is pure, enduring forever.

The ordinances of the Lord are sure, and all of them are righteous.

¹⁰They are more precious than gold, than much pure gold;

they are sweeter than honey, than honey from the honeycomb.

¹¹By them your servant is warned; in keeping them there is great reward.

➜ **THINK** How good are God's guidelines for life? Pick out the words used in this passage to describe them, such as *perfect*. Jot them down here.

God's "laws," "statutes," "commands," and so on sound sensational. But what exactly do they accomplish for you? Look for four things in verses 7 and 8, and a couple more in verse 11.

Now check the price tag on God's insights. What does this passage say about their value?

➜ **LIVE** Totally flawless. Uniquely useful. Insanely valuable. That's what Psalm 19 claims about God's instructions for life. But that begs a big question: Do you believe all that? Why—or why not?

Just so we're clear on a basic point, exactly where do you tap into God's wise words?

Unlike any other source of knowledge, the Bible gets you God's pure wisdom. Not only does it explain how Jesus' death on the cross brings you close to God, but it also tells you God's smart way to live. The apostle Paul puts it like this: "All Scripture is inspired by God and is useful to teach us what is true and to make us realize what is wrong in our lives. It corrects us when we are wrong and teaches us to do what is right. God uses it to prepare and equip his people to do every good work" (2 Timothy 3:16-17, NLT).

How have you used the Bible to figure out your life and make smart choices? How has it worked for you—or not?

➡   **WRAP** No other source of guidance can match the infinite intelligence of the God who knows everything about your world—and about you. No other source of guidance comes close to his unlimited love for your world—and for you. When it comes to getting info on how to get through life, his words are your most valuable and completely reliable resource.

» MORE THOUGHTS TO MULL

- God and his Word aren't the only voice fighting for your attention. Who else tries to tell you how you should do life? How much do you listen to them?

- Name a person you know who does life by the book—the Bible, that is. Why does he or she trust the Bible? How does their biblical wisdom make a difference in real life?

- You can't live by God's Word if it doesn't stay in your mind. Set a goal for how many Bible verses you want to memorize while you work through *Choose*. Tip: You can start with the verses that are highlighted at the beginning of each study.

» MORE SCRIPTURES TO DIG

- Check out the start of **Psalm 19** to catch another way you receive God's wisdom. It says the sky shouts God's glory⊔ his awe-inspiring majesty and splendor, his jaw-dropping perfection and power. God's handiwork in creation, in fact, shows human beings enough about God that we are "without excuse." We can discern that God put us here, that we belong to him, and that we answer to him (**Romans 1:19-20**). There's not a place on earth that doesn't get this info about God.

- The Bible wraps together all of God's words for you to read firsthand. God talked to the human race first through his spokespersons, the prophets (**2 Peter 1:19-22**), then through Jesus. The Bible calls Jesus *the Word* (**John 1:1-14**).

- **Psalm 119** is the longest chapter in the Bible (176 verses!), and it happens to be all about the greatness of God's words. Psalm 19 is like a miniature version of that big Psalm.

4. THE ULTIMATE INSIDE JOB

Good choices start on the inside

Ephesians 4:23-24 (NCV)

But you were taught to be made new in your hearts, to become a new person.

That new person is made to be like God—made to be truly good and holy.

➡️ **START** The moment that word crashes past your lips, you clap your hands over your mouth. Cussing—you've done it again! #@&%*! And now you did it *again!* You press your hands over your mouth even harder, letting go only when you stand alone at the bathroom sink. Your grandpa says his mom scrubbed his mouth with soap whenever he said a bad word. Sure, Great-Grandma used bar soap, but a squirt of liquid soap on your toothbrush should have the same effect. No, you aren't sure it will end your swearing habit. No, you haven't thought about what the soap might do to your innards. But if it was good enough for Great-Grandma, then it's good enough for you....

What do you do when you want to break a bad habit or stop doing a sin?

➡️ **READ** Ephesians 4:17-24 (NCV)

[17]In the Lord's name, I tell you this. Do not continue living like those who do not believe. Their thoughts are worth nothing. [18]They do not understand, and they know nothing, because they refuse to listen. So they cannot have the life that God gives. [19]They have lost all feeling of shame, and they use their lives for doing evil. They continually want to do all kinds of evil. [20]But what you learned in Christ was not like this. [21]I know that you heard about him, and you are in him, so you were taught the truth that is in Jesus. [22]You were taught to leave your old self—to stop living the evil way you lived before. That old self becomes worse, because people are fooled by the evil things they want to do. [23]But you were taught to be made new in your hearts, [24]to become a new person. That new person is made to be like God—made to be truly good and holy.

➜   **THINK** Right off the top, this passage launches into a description of people who don't know God. What's wrong with how they think? How does that affect how they act?

There's something significantly different about people who are connected to God. What are they supposed to do once they meet Jesus?

Think hard about this one: Exactly how does someone become "a new person"?

➜   **LIVE** What habits or sins have you tried to change by attacking the problem with brute force, like a foul-mouthed kid trying to cease his swearing with a squirt of soap?

God aims for you to make great choices in every moment of your life. But he doesn't *force* you to act differently by overpowering you from the outside. He starts by changing your heart, altering how you think and feel. So suppose you constantly say "God!" in a way that isn't exactly prayerful. You could ask a friend to grab your lips and twist them shut every time you "misuse God's name" (Exodus 20:7). Or you could let God remake you from the inside out by asking him for forgiveness, thinking about what it means to respect the Lord, asking God to help you hate wrong and love right, telling him you want to understand the special-ness of his name...*and* begging a friend to poke you when you mess up without thinking.

Think of your worst habit, or a sin that often snags you. How can you tackle that problem not just from the outside, but from the inside as well?

→ **WRAP** God doesn't want you to make good choices so you'll end up feeling miserable. However, you'll only be glad to choose God's best when you let him change your insides. Once you let God rearrange your heart, how you talk and act will start to look different too.

» MORE THOUGHTS TO MULL

- Think again about that bad habit that bugs you. For every "outside" way you've tried to change, brainstorm two "inside" ways to attack the problem.

- When God gets hold of your heart, you do right simply because you want to—not because you have to. Ponder this: In what areas of life do you choose good because it's truly the deepest desire of your heart? How did that happen?

- What does it look like for someone your age to be "truly good and holy," as Ephesians 4:24 (NCV) says?

» MORE SCRIPTURES TO DIG

- Jesus has tough words for the religious teachers of his day because they use brute force to discipline their outsides while letting sin run wild on their insides. He said they're like freshly painted tombs—pretty on the surface, but full of dead people's bones underneath. He said, "You clean the outside of the cup and dish, but inside [you] are full of greed and self-indulgence. Blind Pharisee! First clean the inside of the cup and dish, and then the outside also will be clean" (**Matthew 23:25-26**).

- Here's another deep insight that Jesus tosses at those religious teachers. He says their rotten words come from rotten innards, while good words come from a good heart (**Matthew 12:34-35**). The point for you? Real change starts on the inside.

- Read the rest of **Ephesians 4** and keep on going through **Ephesians 5** to spot the great results you get once you "leave your old self" and are "made new in your hearts" (Ephesians 4:22-23), ditching not only bad behaviors, but also the thickheaded thinking behind them.

5. HELP FOR UNIBROWS

Getting to know God remakes you

Titus 3:4-5

But when the kindness and love of God our Savior appeared, he saved us,

not because of righteous things we had done, but because of his mercy.

He saved us through the washing of rebirth and renewal by the Holy Spirit.

➜   **START** Merely knowing the right thing to do never made anyone do it. We might want to live according to God's wisdom. We might try hard to steer wide of the stupidity of sin. But how does that really happen? There's only one answer: Jesus. A letter that the apostle Paul wrote to his friend Titus tells how to get started. Titus was on the Mediterranean island of Crete, aiming to help the Cretans change. One problem: Cretans had a reputation for being as dumb as stumps. In fact, calling someone a "cretain" today is more or less saying he's a caveman. But God has the power to change even unibrows.

Brainstorm your thoughts: What does Jesus have to do with you becoming a different person?

➜   **READ** Titus 3:3-8

³At one time we too were foolish, disobedient, deceived and enslaved by all kinds of passions and pleasures. We lived in malice and envy, being hated and hating one another. ⁴But when the kindness and love of God our Savior appeared, ⁵he saved us, not because of righteous things we had done, but because of his mercy. He saved us through the washing of rebirth and renewal by the Holy Spirit, ⁶whom he poured out on us generously through Jesus Christ our Savior, ⁷so that, having been justified by his grace, we might become heirs having the hope of eternal life. ⁸This is a trustworthy saying. And I want you to stress these things, so that those who have trusted in God may be careful to devote themselves to doing what is good. These things are excellent and profitable for everyone.

➔   **THINK** Paul expects the Cretans to make good choices in all parts of their lives. He tells Titus, "Remind the believers to yield to the authority of rulers and government leaders, to obey them, to be ready to do good, to speak no evil about anyone, to live in peace, and to be gentle and polite to all people" (Titus 3:1-2, NCV). That's what the Cretans are *supposed* to look like. But that's not where they're at.

When Paul says, "Hey, at one time we too were..." what does that imply the Cretans are like? List a bunch of ugly things the Cretans must have seen whenever they looked in a mirror.

Paul isn't picking on the Cretans. He admits he's a fellow spiritual slob who has discovered a stunning truth: God himself reaches into our lives and rescues us. Not because we've done anything to earn "the kindness and love of God our Savior," but because of his mercy and grace□ his compassion that we don't deserve.

Verses 5-7 string together all kinds of things that happen when Jesus is your Savior. What are they?

It's like this: When you become a Christian—when God saves you—two major things happen. First, you're *reborn* spiritually—made God's child. You're washed clean of your sins—forgiven. You're justified—made right in God's sight. Second, you start to *grow*. You get a new life that starts now and lasts forever in heaven. God begins making fantastic changes in you—that's the "renewal by the Holy Spirit." Your new relationship with God is what makes you able to make the same amazing choices that the Christians living in Crete were about to make.

➜   **LIVE** This Bible passage lays out the facts of what God has done for us. Other spots in the Bible emphasize *our right response to these facts.* We have all done wrong against God. We've all wrecked our relationship with him to the point that we deserve death—eternal separation from him—yet Jesus paid the penalty for our sins. We are made right with God when we accept those facts. In some spots the Bible calls that "having faith." (See Romans 3:22-24.) Here, it's called "trusting in God" (Titus 3:8).

Really big question: Do you trust God?

Maybe you've placed your trust in God ever since you were a small child. Or maybe you remember a specific time and place when you decided you believe in him. If neither of those things sounds true of you, then you can get started on a life-altering relationship with God right now. You can tell him, "God, I've done wrong against you. I know Jesus died in my place for those wrongs—those sins. I accept the forgiveness you can offer me because of what Jesus did for me. And I want to live for you." Believe that? Then grow on.

➜   **WRAP** God can even re-create Cretan cavemen. Trusting in Jesus is the first step to seeing that happen.

» **MORE THOUGHTS TO MULL**

- If you aren't sure you trust in Jesus to make you right with God and make you a new person, why not? Grab a soda or coffee with a Christian friend or youth pastor and talk things through.

- Tell someone what it means to you to have a relationship with God.

- Rethink the question you answered at the start: What does Jesus have to do with you becoming a different person?

» MORE SCRIPTURES TO DIG

- God wants to make you a new person who consistently makes great choices that help you survive and thrive in life. But you don't become a new person in order to win God's love. God already loves us just as we are—that's one of the Bible's most astounding truths. The best-known Bible verse on this topic is **Romans 5:8**: "But God demonstrates his own love for us in this: While we were still sinners, Christ died for us." The reason God saves us—makes us his friends and makes us new—isn't because we deserve his favor. He chooses to love us even when we're unlovable.

- **1 Corinthians 1:30** says Jesus "has become for us wisdom from God." If you want to truly get wise, you need to get Jesus. If you want to steer wide of the stupidity of sin, then you need to stick close to him.

- Check out **Colossians 1:21-23** for a tight description of the facts on what it means to trust in God.

6. SAY NO TO STUPIDITY

God's grace teaches you to say "No!"

Titus 2:11-12

For the grace of God has appeared that offers salvation to all people.

It teaches us to say "No" to ungodliness and worldly passions,

and to live self-controlled, upright and godly lives in this present age.

➜ **START** Standing on the rickety bridge, you look down between your feet—and a hundred feet below you can see a rushing, foaming river that twists through a rocky canyon. You've never been on a see-through bridge before, but standing on these rotten wooden planks and peering through gaping holes, you can see plenty. "It's okay," your friend calls from up ahead. "I've been over it a dozen times." You hesitate. A bit downriver is another bridge. It's brand new, built of concrete, and strong enough for a line of fully loaded trucks to cross over. You want to go with your friend. But you hesitate. You might get away with it once. Or twice. Or even a dozen times. But sooner or later, you'll have a gut-splattering landing on the rocks below.

When have you said yes to doing something stupidly risky or wrong when you'd have been better off saying no?

➜ **READ** Titus 2:11-14

[11]For the grace of God has appeared that offers salvation to all people. [12]It teaches us to say "No" to ungodliness and worldly passions, and to live self-controlled, upright and godly lives in this present age, [13]while we wait for the blessed hope—the appearing of the glory of our great God and Savior, Jesus Christ, [14]who gave himself for us to redeem us from all wickedness and to purify for himself a people that are his very own, eager to do what is good.

➔   **THINK** "Grace" is an enormous Bible idea. It's God's "unmerited favor" toward you. "Salvation" is everything God does to rescue you from sin and build a relationship with you.

What does God's grace train you to say no to? What kind of life does he want you to say yes to?

"Ungodliness" is the attitude that God doesn't matter, along with all the evil actions that result when you ignore God and his commands. "Worldly passions" are cravings to do what's wrong. To be "self-controlled" means to act rightly toward yourself; "upright" is about acting rightly toward others; and "godly" is acting rightly toward God.

What are Christians waiting for? What difference does that make for how we act right now?

Why does God want to free us from "all wickedness"? What's the end result?

➜   **LIVE** How would you explain to your friends why you think it's worth saying no to ungodliness?

What choices between doing right or doing wrong have you faced today? Which way did you go?

How does God's grace help you want to make good choices?

➜   **WRAP** Saying no to unwise choices isn't about avoiding every risk or playing life safe all the time. Following Jesus can be both daring and dangerous. But it means picking the smart path□ one that will show honor to God, love toward others, and respect for yourself. It's choosing to ditch sin and do what's right.

» MORE THOUGHTS TO MULL

- When has a friend tugged you into doing something bad? How could you resist the stupidity of sin the next time that powerful temptation comes your way?

- Does making good choices doom you to a boring life? Explain your answer.

- Ask some Christians who are a few years older than you how they decided they really wanted to follow God.

» MORE SCRIPTURES TO DIG

- **2 Corinthians 5:14-15** describes the impact of God's grace in slightly different language. It says God's love for us makes living for him totally worthwhile. The apostle Paul wrote, "For Christ's love compels us, because we are convinced that one died for all, and therefore all died. And he died for all, that those who live should no longer live for themselves but for him who died for them and was raised again."

- Here's another passage that says God's kindness is what drives you to make good choices. **Romans 12:1** puts it like this: "Therefore, I urge you, brothers and sisters, in view of God's mercy, to offer your bodies as a living sacrifice, holy and pleasing to God—this is true worship." Take a minute and talk to God about that. Try something like this: "God, you are incredibly kind. You are wiser than anyone in this world, including me. You sent your Son to die for me. You forgive me every day. Because of your great mercy, I want to be different. I choose to live for you."

- Read **Joshua 24:14-15**, where Joshua tells a crowd of people that he's going to follow God, no matter what they choose to do.

7. GOALS FOR GROWTH

God's power to change

2 Peter 1:3

His divine power has given us everything we need for a godly life

through our knowledge of him who called us by his own glory and goodness.

➔   **START** God wants to make you smart so you'll understand all he's done for you. But real wisdom never resides just in your brain. In the Bible, genuine wisdom always makes a difference in your daily life. When wisdom gets into your head, love gets into your heart. 1 Corinthians 13:2 says you might be able to "fathom all mysteries and all knowledge," but if you don't have love, then *you are nothing*.

What do you want your faith in Jesus to look like one year from now? In other words, how much will you trust him? In what ways do you want to be a new and better person?

➔   **READ** 2 Peter 1:3-9

³His divine power has given us everything we need for a godly life through our knowledge of him who called us by his own glory and goodness. ⁴Through these he has given us his very great and precious promises, so that through them you may participate in the divine nature, having escaped the corruption in the world caused by evil desires. ⁵For this very reason, make every effort to add to your faith goodness; and to goodness, knowledge; ⁶and to knowledge, self-control; and to self-control, perseverance; and to perseverance, godliness; ⁷and to godliness, mutual affection; and to mutual affection, love. ⁸For if you possess these qualities in increasing measure, they will keep you from being ineffective and unproductive in your knowledge of our Lord Jesus Christ. ⁹But if any of you do not have them, you are nearsighted and blind, and you have forgotten that you have been cleansed from your past sins.

➜   **THINK** What has God's power given you? How does God give you those things?

So what does a grown-up, amazingly mature Christian look like? List the qualities such a person would have.

Your starting point is faith (the trust in God that begins when you first believe). But there's lots more that God wants to build into you: goodness (moral excellence), knowledge (an understanding of God and his plans for you), self-control (the capacity to resist doing wrong), perseverance (the ability to press on in your faith even when it's hard), godliness (paying attention to God in every part of life), mutual affection (fellowship between God's followers), and love (sacrificing for others).

Knowing God and grabbing hold of his promises produces change—but it's a lifelong, ever-expanding transformation. Still, what are you if you're not gaining more and more of those things? What have you forgotten?

➔   **LIVE** When you look at that list of qualities God wants to give you, where would you like to grow first—and most?

Would you be disappointed if you realized a year from now that you don't know God any better—or that your life doesn't look any different? Why or why not?

Being "ineffective" and "unproductive" (verse 8) sounds like no big deal, as if you didn't do enough extra credit at school to rocket a grade into the A-plus zone. But missing out on spiritual growth is a lot worse than that. It can result in the kind of crash-and-burn spiritual life you don't want: feeling distant from God, being trapped in bad choices, having a prayer life that seems pointless, being bored out of your brain in church, always wondering if you're really a Christian.

➔   **WRAP** Spiritual growth doesn't stop with deciding to trust Jesus. Knowing him is meant to remake your life. It's how you live right and stick close to your Savior.

》   MORE THOUGHTS TO MULL

- When have you experienced the biggest spiritual growth in your life? What factors helped that to happen?

- Who do you know that you want to be like—in your own unique way, of course? What qualities of maturity do you see in that person?

- Find an adult—a youth pastor, a parent, or a mentor—who is interested in your long-term spiritual growth. Talk together about how he or she can help you build your faith.

》   MORE SCRIPTURES TO DIG

- These verses from 2 Peter say that if you don't want to grow spiritually, perhaps you've forgotten you've been forgiven. Jesus once pointed out that one of his followers—a former prostitute—was greatly devoted to him because she knew the ghastliness of her sins. "But whoever has been forgiven little," Jesus said, "loves little." Your sins don't have to be gigantic for you to be grateful. Read **Luke 7:36-50** to learn how remembering where you came from—and what God has done for you—helps you grow in gratitude.

- Growing in God isn't something you do on your own. Not only do you need God's power working inside you, but you also need good friends pulling and prodding you along. Look at what **Ephesians 4:11-16** says about how much you need others if you expect to make spiritual progress.

8. KEEP IN STEP

The Holy Spirit grows you

Galatians 5:22-23

But the fruit of the Spirit is love, joy, peace, patience,

kindness, goodness, faithfulness, gentleness and self-control.

Against such things there is no law.

➔ **START** No one has to tell trees to grow. They sip water, absorb nutrients, and bask in the sun, inhaling carbon dioxide and exhaling oxygen. If they're in the right spot, trees grow automatically. That's how your spiritual life is supposed to work. If you're connected to God, you get everything you need to live smart. There's one major point, however, where you differ from a tree: You have legs. Trees bloom where they're planted, but you have to plant yourself where you'll bloom.

How well do you make the most of opportunities to grow spiritually? Explain.

➔ **READ** Galatians 5:19-25

[19]The acts of the sinful nature are obvious: sexual immorality, impurity and debauchery; [20]idolatry and witchcraft; hatred, discord, jealousy, fits of rage, selfish ambition, dissensions, factions [21]and envy; drunkenness, orgies, and the like. I warn you, as I did before, that those who live like this will not inherit the kingdom of God. [22]But the fruit of the Spirit is love, joy, peace, patience, kindness, goodness, faithfulness, [23]gentleness and self-control. Against such things there is no law. [24]Those who belong to Christ Jesus have crucified the sinful nature with its passions and desires. [25]Since we live by the Spirit, let us keep in step with the Spirit.

➔ **THINK** None of us is guilty of everything on that first list—well, probably not. But the "sinful nature" is how we act without God's help, and those items are examples of the actions and attitudes we can expect to see when sin rules us. By the way, when Paul says, "Those who live like this will not inherit the kingdom of God," he isn't talking about Christians who stumble occasionally. The grammar indicates a habit of giving in to sin regularly. People who do those things show they haven't received God's Spirit.

If that's the sort of badness we do on our own, what better stuff does the Holy Spirit grow in us? Jot down a list.

The apostle Paul doesn't explain exactly how that growth happens. But elsewhere in the Bible, you discover that the Holy Spirit gives you new birth (Titus 3:5), teaches you (John 14:26), empowers you (Acts 1:8), and fills you with his Spirit (1 Corinthians 12:7; Ephesians 5:18).

The Spirit changes you in a way that's as natural as a fruit tree sprouting fruit. But there's something for you to do. What is it? Check verse 25.

➜   **LIVE** What kind of good changes do you see the Spirit causing in you?

Make a list of the top five people, hobbies, interests, and situations that occupy your day. Which help you grow good fruit?

What concrete things can you do today—and every day—to "keep in step with the Spirit"? Are you up for that—or not?

➜   **WRAP** The Holy Spirit gives you new life. Now you need to stay close. It's like going for a walk. God is God, so he gets to pick the path. But every time he takes a step, you make the choice to take the same step or to walk the other way. The more you stick with the Holy Spirit, the more he changes you.

» MORE THOUGHTS TO MULL

- The rest of Galatians 5 says there's a battle between right and wrong going on inside each of us. How big is the battle that's raging inside you? Pick one: a) guns and grenades, b) tanks and fighter planes, or c) weapons of mass destruction. Whatever your situation, where can you turn for help?

- When God's Spirit and your sinful nature go to war inside you, who usually wins?

- What's your toughest battle as a Christian? Talk to God about it. Ask him to work inside of you by his Spirit, to strengthen you through his Word, and to help you be wholly devoted to him.

» MORE SCRIPTURES TO DIG

- Just a bit after this Bible passage, Paul writes that when you say yes to the Spirit and obey God, you stay in the right spot for him to grow you some more. Yet when you give in to your sinful nature, you shrivel and die. He put it like this: "Don't be misled—you cannot mock the justice of God. You will always harvest what you plant. Those who live only to satisfy their own sinful nature will harvest decay and death from that sinful nature. But those who live to please the Spirit will harvest everlasting life from the Spirit. So let's not get tired of doing what is good. At just the right time we will reap a harvest of blessing if we don't give up" (**Galatians 6:7-9**, NLT).

- The Holy Spirit might seem hard to understand. But along with the Father and the Son—Jesus—the Spirit is fully God. He's the third "person" in our God, whom the Bible presents as a "trinity" (think "tri-unity"). Jesus promised that when he went back to heaven, the Spirit would come to us as our Counselor or Comforter (**John 14:16-17**). The Holy Spirit is God, and he's always with you. In fact, he's so close that the Bible says he lives inside you (**Romans 8:11**).

9. WATCH OUT!

Standing up to temptation

1 Corinthians 10:12-13

So, if you think you are standing firm, be careful that you don't fall!

No temptation has overtaken you except what is common to us all.

And God is faithful; he will not let you be tempted beyond what you can bear.

But when you are tempted, he will also provide a way out so that you can endure it.

➜   **START** Maybe you always sit in the front row at church. Maybe you have Christian family members, Christian friends, Christian T-shirts, Christian bracelets, Christian music—and you've even convinced your parents to glue a shiny Christian fish to the back of the family car. So what! Actually, those are good things. Some of them are great. But not one of them guarantees your spiritual success. So catch a lesson from this New Testament passage recalling some Old Testament believers who thought they were safe from temptation. Even though they had all the right outward signs of belief, they still were whipped by evil.

If you're a believer committed to doing right, how can you still feel tempted to do wrong?

➜   **READ** 1 Corinthians 10:6-13

⁶Now these things occurred as examples to keep us from setting our hearts on evil things as they did. ⁷Do not be idolaters, as some of them were; as it is written: "The people sat down to eat and drink and got up to indulge in revelry." ⁸We should not commit sexual immorality, as some of them did—and in one day twenty-three thousand of them died. ⁹We should not test Christ, as some of them did—and were killed by snakes. ¹⁰And do not grumble, as some of them did—and were killed by the destroying angel. ¹¹These things happened to them as examples and were written down as warnings for us, on whom the culmination of the ages has come. ¹²So, if you think you are standing firm, be careful that you don't fall! ¹³No temptation has overtaken you except what is common to us all. And God is faithful; he will not let you be tempted beyond what you can bear. But when you are tempted, he will also provide a way out so that you can endure it.

➡   **THINK** Sparing the ugly details, these people were into idol-atry—remember the golden calf?—or worshiping other gods (Exodus 32:1-6); pagan celebrations (Exodus 32:6); sexual immorality, which led to 24,000 deaths (Numbers 25:1-9); testing God, to which God responded with poisonous snakes (Numbers 21:6); and grumbling, which brought on a plague of death (Numbers 14:2, 37).

According to this passage, what attitude almost guarantees that you'll get trounced by temptation?

This passage doesn't just warn you. It gives you an enormous promise. Write that promise here in your own words.

➡   **LIVE** Be honest: What are the chances that at some point you'll stumble big in your Christian life? Why do you think that? And what will keep that from happening?

Being tempted is unavoidable. Being overwhelmed is not. Even Jesus was tempted (Matthew 4:1-11). And the apostle Paul must believe he's not above these warnings because he says these examples are for "us," not "you." If you think you could never fall, watch out.

Think of the biggest temptation you face. What ways of escape has God provided for you?

Paul doesn't say what God's "way out" will look like in every situation. But God promises that it's there. How intensely do you look for his way out of sin? Details, please.

➡   **WRAP**   God's Old Testament people sometimes assumed they were above temptation. Watch out whenever you utter what might become your famous last words before you fall into sin: "That could never happen to me." "I'd never do that." "I'm strong. I can handle this." "I don't feel tempted at all." "It's okay if I do this one little thing."

»   MORE THOUGHTS TO MULL

- When has God given you a way out of sin☐ but you ignored it?

- The apostle Paul is telling you a lot of dirt. Isn't it wrong to study these bad examples? Why—or why not?

- Ask an older Christian to help you find your way of escape from your worst situations. Knowing exactly how to find God's "way out" takes time and wisdom.

» MORE SCRIPTURES TO DIG

- When you feel tempted, know that God understands. This passage is talking about Jesus: "For our high priest is able to understand our weaknesses. He was tempted in every way that we are, but he did not sin. Let us, then, feel very sure that we can come before God's throne where there is grace. There we can receive mercy and grace to help us when we need it" (**Hebrews 4:15-16**, NCV).

- Look at **1 Corinthians 10:1-5** to see the peak spiritual experiences God's Old Testament people enjoyed. They were "under the cloud," experiencing God's guidance. They "passed through the sea," gaining freedom when the Lord rescued them from slavery. They were "baptized into Moses," united to God via one of God's right-hand leaders. Amazingly, they even experienced Christ. These folks had been to all the right concerts, church services, retreats, and mission projects. But look what happened to them. The good news? It doesn't have to be that way.

10. SUBMIT, RESIST, WIN

Your enemy, the Devil

James 4:7

Submit yourselves, then, to God.

Resist the devil, and he will flee from you.

➜ **START** You might think the Devil is a cartoon guy with a closet stocked with pitchforks and red pairs of long undies. Or you might picture him as the terrifying yet fascinating fiend of horror flicks. But the Bible asserts that he's neither. He's your dark and deadly, always active enemy. He wages war against all your efforts to choose God's best.

What do you think the Devil has to do with your fight to do right?

➜ **READ** James 4:7-10

> ⁷Submit yourselves, then, to God. Resist the devil, and he will flee from you. ⁸Come near to God and he will come near to you. Wash your hands, you sinners, and purify your hearts, you double-minded. ⁹Grieve, mourn and wail. Change your laughter to mourning and your joy to gloom. ¹⁰Humble yourselves before the Lord, and he will lift you up.

➜ **THINK** Several people named James pop up in the New Testament, but the author of this Bible book happens to be the brother of Jesus and a chief leader of the church in Jerusalem. He offers some rapid-fire instructions for resisting sin, each in a verb tense that requires an immediate response. List as many as you can find. There are nearly a dozen.

Look at that first thing you should do. What does that mean—and why does it come first?

How are you supposed to act toward the author of all evil, the Devil? What will happen if you heed that command?

The Devil doesn't force you to sin. But he and his cronies spend day and night selling you on the idea. Not only does James say you need to "resist the devil," but Peter also warns you: "Your enemy the devil prowls around like a roaring lion looking for someone to devour" (1 Peter 5:8). And the Devil himself showed up to tempt Jesus face to face at the start of Jesus' public ministry (Matthew 4:1-11).

➜   **LIVE** Those instructions from James sound like tough slogging against sin. Which is the hardest for you to do? How come?

Verse 9 hits us right in the heart. It says to "grieve" (a strong word that means "to be miserable"), "mourn" (show "passionate grief"), and "wail" ("outward grief"). We're to flip "laughter to mourning" and "joy to gloom." The point isn't to be a perpetually gloomy Christian but to be serious about the sins we've committed, seeing and grieving their true badness and turning away from them totally. James urges us to get sad, but get over it☐ not by brushing off our sins, but by going to God for forgiveness and help in getting rid of the habits that hurt us.

So if you do those things, what will God do? How do you feel about that?

The next time temptation hits you, what are you going to do?

➜ **WRAP** Temptation is something that wells up from within— you can check that out in James 1:13-14—but it's also as if you're getting pelted with rocks and garbage from the outside. The secret to your success is this: "So give yourselves completely to God. Stand against the devil, and the devil will run from you" (James 4:7, NCV).

» MORE THOUGHTS TO MULL

- To "purify your hearts" from being "double-minded" means you decide that you really hate sin. Is that where you're at? Why—or why not?

- Do you see temptation as an opportunity to grow up—or to give up and get dragged into evil?

- Christian author C. S. Lewis wrote in *The Screwtape Letters*, "There are two equal and opposite errors into which our race can fall about the devils. One is to disbelieve in their existence. The other is to believe, and to feel an excessive and unhealthy interest in them. They themselves are equally pleased by both errors." Which are you more likely to do—believe the Devil has nothing to do with your fight against evil? Or believe he's too powerful for you to overcome?

» MORE SCRIPTURES TO DIG

- Study how Jesus counted on the facts of Scripture to battle temptation in **Matthew 4:1-11**.

- God wants you to have some serious sorrow about sin, but he doesn't want you to stay there. Read this passage and commit it to memory. It starts with some bad news, followed by really good news: "If we say we have no sin, we are fooling ourselves, and the truth is not in us. But if we confess our sins, he will forgive our sins, because we can trust God to do what is right. He will cleanse us from all the wrongs we have done" (**1 John 1:8-9,** NCV).

- Don't go to bed scared of the Devil. Check what **1 John 4:4** says. It's all about God living in you—the God who has the power to kick the Devil's tail.

11. LISTEN UP—OR NOT

Shutting out evil voices

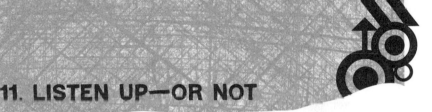

Proverbs 2:12 (NLT)

Wisdom will save you from evil people,

from those whose words are twisted.

➜   **START** The Devil probably doesn't climb into your world the same way he did with Jesus—showing up personally to lure you into evil. Real-life tempters usually have familiar faces, whether they be friends you know up close or celebrities you only gaze at from a distance. They might shout at you. They might whisper. They might be clearly evil, or they might be masquerading as good. Whatever their approach, they want to drag you into doing the same wrong stuff they do.

Let's assume you don't say yes to every invitation to ditch good and go wicked. So what's your secret for resisting offers to do bad?

➜   **READ** Proverbs 2:12-15 (NLT)

> [12]Wisdom will save you from evil people,
> from those whose words are twisted.
> [13]These men turn from the right way
> to walk down dark paths.
> [14]They take pleasure in doing wrong,
> and they enjoy the twisted ways of evil.
> [15]Their actions are crooked,
> and their ways are wrong.

➜   **THINK** Read between the lines of that passage: Exactly how does wisdom save you from evil people?

How can you spot a bad guy—or a bad girl, for that matter? List some key characteristics.

The definition of *evil* isn't fuzzy. It literally means "unpleasant, bringing pain and misery." Try inserting that phrase where the verse says "evil."

What makes evil people happy?

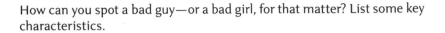 **LIVE** You might be thinking, *Nobody but a mass murderer fits that description.* But plenty of people speak twisted words...choose wrong instead of right...sneak around behind the backs of parents, teachers, and other adults...and enjoy doing bad. Who in your immediate circle has the potential to lead you astray, even in small ways?

How do evil-doing people influence you? (Note: The question doesn't ask, "*Do* those people influence you?" The issues are "How?" and "How much?")

One last blunt question: What things do *you* do that encourage others to choose anything less than God's best? What will you do about that?

→   **WRAP** You've heard countless lectures about peer pressure, and surely you're no dummy when it comes to blocking out voices that entice you to wild sin. But think hard about the countless times each day when you're encouraged by others to choose less than God's very best. Sometimes it's the people with warm smiles and familiar faces who lead you away from God little by little.

» MORE THOUGHTS TO MULL

- How do your peers and other people encourage you to make good choices?

- Think about your tightest circle of friends. Are you influencing them or are they influencing you? What's your proof? And how are you helping each other choose to do good things?

- How do voices from media, sports, fashion, music, and so on influence the choices you make?

» MORE SCRIPTURES TO DIG

- Read **Proverbs 1** for reasons to plug your ears to bad voices. Then read **Proverbs 3** for encouragement to listen to people who can make you wise.

- **2 Timothy 2:22** tells you the best kind of friends to let into your life: "Flee the evil desires of youth and pursue righteousness, faith, love and peace, along with those who call on the Lord out of a pure heart."

- You might be smart, but don't ever think you're immune to peer pressure. Give **Matthew 26:31-35** a read, followed by **Matthew 26:69-75**, and you'll see that even the strongest believers sometimes cave to peer fear. Watch out!

12. YOU'RE IN CHARGE

Staying in control

Ephesians 5:15

Be very careful, then, how you live—

not as unwise but as wise.

➜ **START** If you ever want a list of all the things God wants to change in your life as he builds you into a new person, check out Ephesians 4:25–5:7. Writing to his close friends at Ephesus□ a city in what is now Turkey—the apostle Paul rattles off a bunch of ways God wants us to choose right. Then he sums up his points with words that might surprise you. He tells you to be careful—and in control.

Suppose you woke up tomorrow and suddenly realized you were in total control of every part of your life. What would you do all day?

➜ **READ** Ephesians 5:15-18

¹⁵Be very careful, then, how you live—not as unwise but as wise, ¹⁶making the most of every opportunity, because the days are evil. ¹⁷Therefore do not be foolish, but understand what the Lord's will is. ¹⁸Do not get drunk on wine, which leads to debauchery. Instead, be filled with the Spirit.

➜ **THINK** Look through that short passage again. What all are you supposed to do? Jot down at least seven commands.

There's a lot packed into that brief chunk. You're to "be careful," giving total attention to how you act. The verb that's translated as "live" literally means how you "walk around." You're to make the most of every "opportunity," a word that describes a seller taking an item off the market, as though you've discovered that your life is too valuable to waste on anything evil. You don't want to be "foolish," a strong word for "stupid." Instead, you'll want to think hard so you can grasp what God wants you to do.

After all of that, Paul throws in the command: "Do not get drunk on wine." Is that random? Why would he mention that here?

Getting sloshed leads to "debauchery," a sort of wasting away or fizzling into nothingness. It's the exact opposite of being in charge of your life—careful, wise, and astute in how you spend your time, while seeing the big picture of God's plan for you.

What's the last command—and why does that matter?

→   **LIVE** Let's go back to that very first question about what you'd do if you were in charge. It's a trick question, actually, because you're already in charge of how you spend every moment of every day. Parents might tell you what to do, and teachers might dictate a big part of your day. But you—and only you—are in control of how you think and act in every moment of life.

Do you buy that? Why—or why not?

How do you feel now that you know God wants you to take charge of your life—not so you can do evil, but in order to do his good will?

As you "walk around" each day, how careful are you? That is, how much do you think about whether you're making wise choices that fit with God's plan for you?

➜   **WRAP** Only you can choose to do what God wants you to do. Whether you realize it or not, you're the only person who's truly running your life.

» MORE THOUGHTS TO MULL

- When do you feel as though you aren't in charge of your life? Make a list of ways that you're indeed in control of how you think or act in those situations.

- Maybe you'd rather do life as a little kid does, always getting taken care of by your parents and other grown-ups. How is that fun—or not?

- How can you be in control of your life without being uptight?

» MORE SCRIPTURES TO DIG

- I've already mentioned that the verb that gets translated as "live" in verse 15 literally means "to walk around." Paul uses that same word four other times in Ephesians 4 and 5. Check the other spots in **Ephesians 4:1**; **4:17**; **5:2** and **5:8** and find out more about how God wants you to stroll through life.

- The fact that God expects you to take charge of your life might be news to you. But the concept of self-control weaves throughout the Bible. It's the grand finale of the fruit of the Spirit you read about in **Galatians 5:22-23**. Without self-control, you're "like a city whose walls are broken down" (**Proverbs 25:28**, NCV). And being "self-controlled and alert" is how you defend yourself against the Devil (**1 Peter 5:8**, NIV). You can discover more of what the Bible has to say about self-control in **1 Thessalonians 5:8**; **1 Timothy 3:2**; **Titus 1:8**; **Titus 2:12**; and **1 Peter 1:13**.

- Look at **Titus 2:1-6** where the apostle Paul tells every kind of believer they need a big dose of self-control.

13. FRESH START

Getting up after you mess up

Philippians 3:13-14

One thing I do: Forgetting what is behind and straining toward what is ahead,

I press on toward the goal to win the prize

for which God has called me heavenward in Christ Jesus.

➜   **START** Spiritually speaking, the apostle Paul was the man. He had every reason to be proud, including the right ethnic heritage, a good education, and super-religious accomplishments. Yet he argues that they're all worthless. When compared to knowing Jesus, they're all "rubbish," "worthless trash," or to be more vivid—"dung" (Philippians 3:8). Yet this intense follower of Jesus still thinks he has plenty of room to grow spiritually. In fact, even Paul had to find a way to get past his failures.

How do you pick yourself up and go on when you've done something wrong?

➜   **READ** Philippians 3:12-14

¹²Not that I have already obtained all this, or have already arrived at my goal, but I press on to take hold of that for which Christ Jesus took hold of me. ¹³Brothers and sisters, I do not consider myself yet to have taken hold of it. But one thing I do: Forgetting what is behind and straining toward what is ahead, ¹⁴I press on toward the goal to win the prize for which God has called me heavenward in Christ Jesus.

➜   **THINK** Right before this passage, Paul describes the amazing experience of totally following God. But he knows he isn't always able to do that. When Paul realizes his relationship with God isn't perfect, what does he do to press on?

What prize does Paul see at the end of his tough run?

➔   **LIVE** Maybe you never mess up. Maybe you've never sinned since the day you decided to follow Jesus. But if you're honest with yourself, you've probably made some mistakes. When sin builds a wall between you and God, how can you break it down and put your friendship with God back together?

What if your failures happened more than once? What would keep you from getting frustrated and giving up?

Paul knows there is nothing better in life than obeying God completely. He knows God wants nothing less than a lifetime of choosing to go God's way. But Paul was able to move past the bad things he did because he knew God's love doesn't depend on him being perfect. Back in Philippians 3:9, in fact, Paul says the only reason he gets along with God is because Jesus died for his sins. Paul says his own task is to own up to those sins, grab hold of God's forgiveness, and get back to living a new life.

Proverbs 28:13 says, "If you hide your sins, you will not succeed. If you confess and reject them, you will receive mercy" (NCV). So how should you talk to God when you've done wrong?

➡   **WRAP** Getting honest about your sins, telling God what you've done, and saying thanks for his forgiveness is how you get up and go on—forgetting what's behind and pushing toward what's ahead. Remember this: Real Christians aren't people who never fall down. They're the ones who get up and keep going.

》   MORE THOUGHTS TO MULL

- How tough is it for you to admit that you do wrong and need forgiveness? Explain.

- How easily do you accept God's forgiveness? Or do you keep beating yourself up for being bad?

- Ask an older Christian how he or she developed a habit of confession. How does that person not only own up to sin, but also get over it?

» MORE SCRIPTURES TO DIG

- Back up and read the background to this passage in **Philippians 3:1-11**.

- Here's a picture of how God deals with your sins. Make a list of the things you know you've done wrong. Tell God you're sorry. Explain that you don't want to do those things anymore and ask him to help you get up and go on. Then crumple up your list and toss it in the trash. Wave good-bye to those sins when the garbage truck comes because that's how God sees it: "He has taken our sins away from us as far as the east is from west" (**Psalm 103:12,** NCV).

- It's tough to feel trapped by sins over and over again. But God has mercy for you every time you need it. See what **Matthew 18:21-35** says about our need to forgive others. If God expects us to be so merciful, think how much more he will show his kind forgiveness to us!

14. LIVE BOLD

Being fearless

Matthew 10:28

Do not be afraid of those who kill the body but cannot kill the soul.

➜   **START** It's a fact that people who choose to live all-out for God sometimes get hassled for that decision. In the tenth chapter of Matthew, Jesus prepares his 12 closest followers to go out and teach that "the kingdom of heaven is near" (Matthew 10:7). He warns these newbie preachers that they'll be adored by some people and thrashed by others. But he tells them that even if they get in trouble with kings and governors, God will give them the right words to speak (Matthew 10:19-20). In this passage the people who "kill the body" represent a range of folks determined to rough up followers of Jesus. Even in the face of these deadly persecutors, the disciples had reasons to be fearless.

When has choosing to do the right thing caused you grief?

➜   **READ** Matthew 10:28-33

Jesus said: [28]"Do not be afraid of those who kill the body but cannot kill the soul. Rather, be afraid of the One who can destroy both soul and body in hell. [29]Are not two sparrows sold for a penny? Yet not one of them will fall to the ground outside your Father's care. [30]And even the very hairs of your head are all numbered. [31]So don't be afraid; you are worth more than many sparrows. [32]Whoever publicly acknowledges me, I will also acknowledge before my Father in heaven. [33]But whoever publicly disowns me I will disown before my Father in heaven."

➜   **THINK** What's the absolute worst that can happen if people don't like you, your right choices, or your Christian beliefs?

That's all they can do? Big relief, huh? Not really? Well, if that's bad, what happens to those who reject God?

How does God show his care when you belong to him?

You might figure God has bigger things to do than number your hairs. But he's not just counting tiles on the ceiling during a boring class. The point is that God's care for you extends beyond major life-or-death issues. Even the smallest details about you matter to him.

➜ **LIVE** How do people treat you when they find out you're a Christian who tries your best to live for Jesus?

Suppose you face a decision that puts you in an uncomfortable spot☐ caught between what friends want you to do and what God expects you to do. Honestly, which side do you usually choose? Why?

When have you been bold about what you believe? What happened?

God wants you to be unafraid about being up front about your faith, but that doesn't mean you should be obnoxious. The boldest disciple of all, Peter, wrote this: "In your hearts revere Christ as Lord. Always be prepared to give an answer to everyone who asks you to give the reason for the hope that you have. But do this with gentleness and respect" (1 Peter 3:15).

➜   **WRAP** Making unpopular choices because you believe in Jesus can be several notches beyond scary. But Proverbs 29:25 (NCV) says "Being afraid of people can get you into trouble, but if you trust the Lord, you will be safe." God told his early disciples☐ and Christians of all times☐ that when they're put to the test, he's right there with them. Trust that. God wants to get rid of your fear.

»   MORE THOUGHTS TO MULL

- When do you get queasy telling others that you live for God? How can you get over that?

- If you could get your peers to understand one fact about what it means to you to follow Jesus, what would it be?

- Some believers around the world suffer far more for their faith than most of us can begin to imagine. To learn more about persecuted Christians worldwide and how you can help them, visit www.opendoors.com.

» MORE SCRIPTURES TO DIG

- The Bible says, "Whoever rejects the Son will not see life, for God's wrath remains on him" (**John 3:36**). That's scary stuff. Yet if you're a Christian, you don't have to fear God's judgment. Here's why: "At one time you were separated from God. You were his enemies in your minds, and the evil things you did were against God. But now God has made you his friends again. He did this through Christ's death in the body so that he might bring you into God's presence as people who are holy, with no wrong, and with nothing of which God can judge you guilty" (**Colossians 1:21-22**, NCV).

- Part of truly following Jesus is speaking truthfully about your belief in him. **Romans 10:9** says, "If you confess with your mouth, 'Jesus is Lord,' and believe in your heart that God raised him from the dead, you will be saved" (NIV). But knowing exactly how and when to speak up doesn't come automatically. One wise Christian said that what a public "confession of faith" looks like "will vary in boldness, fluency, wisdom, sensitivity, and frequency from believer to believer." You often learn only through trial and error what it means to be bold without being bossy.

15. THE BEST NEST

Getting along at home

Ephesians 6:1

Children, obey your parents in the Lord, for this is right.

➡ **START** When you choose to steer wide of the stupidity of sin, God starts his work on your insides, rearranging your attitudes so you think and feel like him. After all, your behaviors start in the heart, and the person you are on the inside is the person you become on the outside. When you follow Jesus wholeheartedly, God doesn't just remix your mind. He challenges how you act on the outside, the concrete choices you make as you get along with people in your life like parents, the opposite sex, people in charge of you, even your enemies. Let's look at parents first.

What do you think God has to do with you getting along with your parents?

➡ **READ** Ephesians 6:1-4

¹Children, obey your parents in the Lord, for this is right. ²"Honor your father and mother"—which is the first commandment with a promise— ³"so that it may go well with you and that you may enjoy long life on the earth." ⁴Fathers, do not exasperate your children; instead, bring them up in the training and instruction of the Lord.

➡ **THINK** You might not like being told to obey your mom and pop or being addressed with the word *children*. Yet you should be flattered by the fact that God shoots his commands straight to you. He assumes that youth and parents should learn side by side and that you're adult enough to hear his instructions. He doesn't tell moms and dads, "Go home and tell your kids to shape up." Yeah, God has some instructions just for you as well as a few words for your parents. It's his wisdom on how to get along.

What command do you bump into right at the start of the passage?

Why do that? And what's the promise if you do obey?

So if that's your job, what duty do your parents get? What should they avoid doing?

➔   **LIVE** What do you like about your relationship with your parents?

How do you struggle with your parents?

Where do you suppose your parents struggle with you?

Suppose your parents aren't strong Christians...or they're not Christians at all. Or maybe you just think they're clueless. In that case, you might wonder if you have an out to do whatever you want. Unless your parents are abusive or directly contradicting God's commands, your duty is still to obey them. Their authority in your life doesn't depend on their knowing God, but on the fact that God gave them the job of guiding you when they gave birth to you.

➔   **WRAP** Growing up isn't a chance to escape the control of your parents. It's your chance to follow God for yourself.

»   MORE THOUGHTS TO MULL

- How do you feel about the fact that God made parents the boss of you?

- What can you do today to help your parents do their job?

- Make time to talk with your parents about areas where you struggle to obey them—or where you think you've demonstrated the responsibility that sometimes earns more freedom. If you frequently knock heads with your parents, find a wise older Christian who can help you be honest about your own shortcomings and figure out how to present your case respectfully.

» MORE SCRIPTURES TO DIG

- The Bible presents obedience to your parents as not just a good idea, but also as, well, a duty. It's the right thing to do. And **Colossians 3:20** explains the extent to which you're to obey: "Children, obey your parents in everything, for this pleases the Lord." The Bible word for *obey* means being ready to hear and carry out instructions, and the grammar shows that action is to be a habit. One more thing: Obeying "in the Lord" means your parents also answer to God.

- The New Century Version of the Bible words a similar Bible chunk like this: "Fathers, do not nag your children. If you are too hard to please, they may want to stop trying" (**Colossians 3:21**). So what do you do if your parents provoke you? The Bible doesn't say exactly, but Paul once gave this advice to Timothy: "Never speak harshly to an older man, but appeal to him respectfully as you would to your own father" (**1 Timothy 5:1**, NLT). If you're in a disagreement with a parent, start by losing the harshness. Then try to make your point more appealing by the amount of respect you show.

- Read **Luke 2:41-52** for a glimpse of how Jesus got along with his parents. Look at how he thought for himself, yet managed to obey his parents the way God commands.

16. MAKER'S DESIGN

God on love and sex

1 Thessalonians 4:3-4

It is God's will that you should be sanctified:

that you should avoid sexual immorality;

that each of you should learn to control your own body

in a way that is holy and honorable

➜   **START** Sex wasn't invented yesterday. If you doubt the Bible has anything to say about sexuality, get informed about what was going on when it was written. Believers were surrounded by people who made sex a religious rite, and the temples were staffed with prostitutes for so-called worship. But these believers broke free from huge sexual sin, including affairs, incest, premarital sex, and homosexuality. When you're trying to make wise choices in your guy-girl relationships, the Bible has loads of information.

If God sat you down and gave you "The Talk" about sex, what would he say?

➜   **READ** 1 Thessalonians 4:3-8

[3]It is God's will that you should be sanctified: that you should avoid sexual immorality; [4]that each of you should learn to control your own body in a way that is holy and honorable, [5]not in passionate lust like the pagans, who do not know God; [6]and that in this matter no one should wrong or take advantage of a brother or sister. The Lord will punish all those who commit such sins, as we told you and warned you before. [7]For God did not call us to be impure, but to live a holy life. [8]Therefore, anyone who rejects this instruction does not reject a human being but God, the very God who gives you his Holy Spirit.

➜   **THINK** "Justification" happens when God declares you not guilty of your sins because you've placed your trust in Jesus. "Sanctification" is the growth that happens after that. To "sanctify" means to "make holy," to "dedicate to God," to "set apart." It's the process of living more and more for God, getting smart, and steering wide of the stupidity of sin.

So what should you avoid? What are you supposed to control?

"Control your own body" can also be translated as "live with your own wife" or "acquire a wife." The point is the same: What the Bible calls "sexual immorality" is out of bounds. Back in the Old Testament, God uttered his command that "You shall not commit adultery" (Exodus 20:14)⬜ that is, you should not have sexual relations outside of marriage. The term *sexual immorality* is even broader, including sex before marriage and all other types of sexual sin.

What does controlling your body look like? How do you know if you're out of control?

The kind of purity God wants to build in you doesn't just show up in behavior ("avoid sexual immorality"). It's also about your attitudes ("passionate lust"). Lust is the hot pursuit of something you can't have—whether it's the right thing at the wrong time or just the wrong thing. God has all the bases covered.

➜   **LIVE** So why choose to stay within God's bounds and save all varieties of sexual closeness for marriage?

Think about your right-now attitudes toward the opposite sex. Do you want what God wants, or are you heading out of bounds? Why?

Suppose you want to make God's good choice to stay sexually pure—both before and within marriage. Who helps you stick to that choice?

➜   **WRAP** God doesn't want to dunk all your bodily desires in ice water. He just wants them to heat up when and where he intended. God designed sex to be hotter than a nuclear-powered toaster. But he wants it to be saved and shared between only a husband and wife. It's part of his plan for them to experience physical and emotional union (Genesis 2:22-24 and Hebrews 13:4).

» MORE THOUGHTS TO MULL

- Do you think God makes commands about sex just to spoil our fun? Why—or why not?

- Write a letter to yourself in which you commit to stay pure. Include the boundaries, reasons for staying pure, and what you'll do to get help if the temptation gets to be too much.

- Sex within a marriage is God's best. And he wants you to run away from the rest: Sex isn't for people who aren't married to each other. It isn't a party game, a dare, or a contest to get as much as you can. The sex God invented isn't selfish, hurtful, violent, or controlling. Sex isn't something adults or teenagers do to children; nor is it for people of the same sex to share. Sex isn't a spectator sport for movie screens and magazines. So decide now: Do you want God's best? If not, you're going to slide into the rest.

» MORE SCRIPTURES TO DIG

- Think God knows nothing about sex? Read **Proverbs 5:15-23** for your Maker's great idea of married love.

- "Lust" is sinful desire, wanting something you can't have. See what Jesus says about it in **Matthew 5:27-30**.

- Just a year or two before Paul wrote this letter to the Thessalonian believers, major leaders of the Early Church had gathered in Jerusalem to decide the major points to teach new Christians. They issued two important instructions. One of them was that believers must flee sexual sin (**Acts 15:22-35**). In other words, out of a world of issues they could have fretted over, they singled out sex as being really important.

17. HOW THEY ROLL

Submitting to authority

Romans 13:1

Let everyone be subject to the governing authorities.

➔   **START** The book of Romans contains some of the Bible's most profound passages on how to get along with God—statements about who he is and how he acts. It's where you find monumental verses such as, "For all have sinned and fall short of the glory of God" (3:23), and "For the wages of sin is death, but the gift of God is eternal life in Christ Jesus our Lord" (6:23). It's the book that says to "Offer your bodies as living sacrifices, holy and pleasing to God—this is your spiritual act of worship" (12:1). Romans is jammed with big ideas. But in chapter 13, the apostle Paul veers into life's nitty-gritty, dealing with police officers and principals. Not that Paul specifically names those people, but you'll get the idea.

Who is someone in charge of some part of your life that you have a tough time obeying?

➔   **READ** Romans 13:1-5

¹Let everyone be subject to the governing authorities, for there is no authority except that which God has established. The authorities that exist have been established by God. ²Consequently, whoever rebels against the authority is rebelling against what God has instituted, and those who do so will bring judgment on themselves. ³For rulers hold no terror for those who do right, but for those who do wrong. Do you want to be free from fear of the one in authority? Then do what is right and you will be commended. ⁴For the one in authority is God's servant for your good. But if you do wrong, be afraid, for rulers do not bear the sword for no reason. They are God's servants, agents of wrath to bring punishment on the wrongdoer. ⁵Therefore, it is necessary to submit to the authorities, not only because of possible punishment but also as a matter of conscience.

➡   **THINK** Who is an authority in your life? What does it mean to submit?

Follow this reasoning: If authority comes from God and you rebel against an authority in your life, then whom are you really rebelling against? What's the consequence of that choice?

Authority in the Bible can be a thing—the right to exercise control—or a person who has power over others. Either way, the Bible says authority is a core characteristic of God, and people only possess authority when God gives it to them.

Why should you submit? Name two good reasons.

Sure, you submit to authority because you don't like blaring sirens. To defy some laws means death, a deterrent that keeps most people in line. Yet punishment isn't the only reason you submit. Your conscience recognizes the structures God puts in place. Without leaders containing us, we'd clobber each other; and the only thing worse than living in a world where everyone seems to boss you around is living in a world where no one does.

➔   **LIVE** How much do you like the Bible's command to submit to authority? Explain.

When have you rebelled when you should have submitted?

➔   **WRAP** As much as we might dislike people who rule us, God put them in our lives for a purpose. We seldom have a real reason to scrap what they want us to do. We're far more likely to disobey merely for the chance to make our own choices.

≫   MORE THOUGHTS TO MULL

- Really, what good are authorities? Make a list of how specific authorities in your life help you. What would your world be like with no authorities?

- Should you fear people who hold positions of power over you? Why—or why not?

- Just for a day, keep track of any times your skin crawls because someone in authority over you—parents, bosses, coaches, teachers—makes you do something.

» MORE SCRIPTURES TO DIG

- Just because this Bible chunk says authority comes from God, that doesn't mean the Bible is ignorant about the nasty qualities of some human authorities. Religious rulers, after all, plotted to do away with Jesus; Roman government officials stood by and permitted him to suffer unjustly; and Roman soldiers carried out the orders to crucify (**Matthew 26:1-5, 27:1-31**). When Jesus faced these evil rulers, however, his response was shocking. He prayed, "Father, forgive them, for they do not know what they are doing" (**Luke 23:34**).

- Believers sometimes face situations where they have no choice but to disobey people in charge. Daniel wouldn't pray to King Darius— and he was almost fed to hungry lions (**Daniel 6**). Shadrach, Meshach, and Abednego refused to bow to an idol—and they were tossed into a hot furnace (**Daniel 3**). Peter kept on preaching when the religious rulers told him to stop—and he was thrown in prison again and again (**Acts 4:1-22; 12:1-5**). Each man refused to comply with ungodly orders. But by accepting the consequences of their "rebellion," they still upheld the concept of authority. Church history shows that many Christians followed Paul's advice and refused to revolt against the government—even in the face of torture and murder. Paul's words weren't cheap: He likely died at the hands of evil authorities.

18. HOW TO BEAT EVIL

Dealing with cruel people

Romans 12:21

Do not be overcome by evil,

but overcome evil with good.

➔ **START** In 33 years of life on earth, Jesus met up with all the cruelty humanity could muster. He suffered insults, personal attacks, and threats on his life—threats that ultimately came to pass at his crucifixion. Incredibly, he didn't strike back with unkindness: "When they hurled their insults at him, he did not retaliate; when he suffered, he made no threats" (1 Peter 2:23). Just as incredibly, God expects the same behavior from us (1 Peter 2:21). Here's what Jesus-like actions toward your enemies look like.

How do you react when a friend or enemy turns cruel on you? Do you usually hold back—or hit back?

➔ **READ** Romans 12:14, 17-21

> [14]Bless those who persecute you; bless and do not curse.... [17]Do not repay anyone evil for evil. Be careful to do what is right in the eyes of everyone. [18]If it is possible, as far as it depends on you, live at peace with everyone. [19]Do not take revenge, my dear friends, but leave room for God's wrath, for it is written: "It is mine to avenge; I will repay," says the Lord. [20]On the contrary: "If your enemy is hungry, feed him; if he is thirsty, give him something to drink. In doing this, you will heap burning coals on his head." [21]Do not be overcome by evil, but overcome evil with good.

➔ **THINK** Recall that *blessed* more or less means "happy." What do you think about trying to help your enemies find joy?

Name four things this passage says you can do in response to the people who make your life miserable.

      Do not...

      Be careful to...

      As far as it depends on you...

      Do not...

Why choose to act like that?

If you refuse to take revenge, what does God promise to do?

➜   **LIVE** An enemy might be a good friend gone bad or someone who attacks at every opportunity. How would you expect either kind of enemy to respond if you acted on the commands in this passage?

Does refusing to take revenge guarantee that you'll get a physical or emotional thrashing? Why—or why not?

The next time someone takes a chunk out of you, how will you respond?

➜ **WRAP** The Bible doesn't promise that every enemy you bless will fall at your feet and beg to be your friend. After all, Jesus offered specific instructions on how to confront evil (Matthew 18:15-17). Yet doing right by your enemies boosts the possibility of good coming out of bad. Choosing to bless your enemies feels strange. But you're trusting God to do his thing.

» MORE THOUGHTS TO MULL

- Have you ever surprised an enemy with kindness? What happened?

- Picture your worst enemy. What three kind things could you do for that person? Pick one and do it.

- In your wildest dreams☐ what's the best possible result you might expect from blessing an enemy?

≫   MORE SCRIPTURES TO DIG

- Choosing to trust God with a bad situation doesn't mean the Lord will step in and deal with your enemy right away. God's holiness means he's wholly against sin. Fortunately for *all* of us, God's wrath is his last resort. God isn't eager to roast evildoers; he's ready to take each of us back into a relationship with him. Peter wrote, "He is patient with you, not wanting anyone to perish, but everyone to come to repentance" (**2 Peter 3:9**). He tells us our job is to do good—even to our enemies. We are to leave the job of judgment to him—with his perfect knowledge and justice.

- Paul didn't invent the idea of being kind to your persecutors. Jesus himself said, "You have heard that it was said, 'Love your neighbor and hate your enemy.' But I tell you, love your enemies and pray for those who persecute you" (**Matthew 5:43-44**).

- Read **2 Peter 1:22-25** for more about how Jesus reacted to people who hated him.

19. LOOK AND LEARN

Don't just read God's Word—do it

James 1:22

Do not merely listen to the word, and so deceive yourselves.

Do what it says.

➜ **START** You wouldn't think of leaving the house in the morning without taking a good look in a mirror. Not only that, but you wouldn't dream of heading out without doing something about what you saw—combing out the bed head, brushing away the fuzz mouth, and doing whatever you do to fix your face. There's a deep spiritual lesson in all of that.

Why do you bother to look in a mirror?

➜ **READ** James 1:22-25

22Do not merely listen to the word, and so deceive yourselves. Do what it says. 23Those who listen to the word but do not do what it says are like people who look at their faces in a mirror 24and, after looking at themselves, go away and immediately forget what they look like. 25But those who look intently into the perfect law that gives freedom and continue in it—not forgetting what they have heard but doing it—they will be blessed in what they do.

➜ **THINK** That verb James uses for "look in a mirror" doesn't refer to a quick glance at yourself as you head out the door. It means to carefully study a subject—in this case, your face. So how is reading the Bible like looking in a mirror?

What are you supposed to do after looking in the mirror of God's Word?

If you don't do that, what are you really doing?

What does God promise will happen if you peer hard into God's Word and do something about what you see?

➜ **LIVE** When have you read the Bible and realized you needed some fixing?

How do you feel about the fact that reading the Bible tells you straight up about your less-than-beautiful features?

Reading the Bible and seeing yourself as you really are can be tough to take. Yet the point of the Bible isn't just to point out your flaws. Over and over it encourages you with words like "For we are God's masterpiece" (Ephesians 2:10, NLT) and "You made my whole being; you formed me in my mother's body. I praise you because you made me in an amazing and wonderful way. What you have done is wonderful. I know this very well" (Psalm 139:13-14, NCV).

How can you make sure you don't forget to apply what you read in God's Word to your everyday life?

➜   **WRAP** Looking in the mirror doesn't make any difference if you don't do something about what you see. Studying God's Word doesn't do you any good if you don't let it change the choices you make.

» MORE THOUGHTS TO MULL

- What's the worst thing about how you look first thing in the morning? How do you remedy that? How much effort do you put into fixing the parts of your life that might look like a mess?

- When have you tried to block out the Bible's teachings because they meant you'd have to change something about your life?

- It's tough to crack open the Bible if you know it's going to tell you that you're doing something wrong. When you feel like that, you need a friend who will hold up the mirror of God's Word so you can see the real you. Whom will you allow to do that?

» MORE SCRIPTURES TO DIG

- A passage mentioned back in Study 3 is worth reading again, just in case you missed it. This time make sure you notice the last sentence, which points out why God uses the Bible to correct us: "All Scripture is inspired by God and is useful to teach us what is true and to make us realize what is wrong in our lives. It corrects us when we are wrong and teaches us to do what is right. God uses it to prepare and equip his people to do every good work" (**2 Timothy 3:16-17,** NLT).

- Sometimes when we look into the mirror of God's Word, our view is blurred by our stubborn resistance to what God wants to show us. Here's a prayer to pray whenever you open God's Book. It's like putting on glasses or contacts to correct your spiritual eyesight: "Search me, God, and know my heart; test me and know my anxious thoughts. See if there is any offensive way in me, and lead me in the way everlasting" (**Psalm 139:23-24**).

20. PRESS ON

Running hard like Jesus

Hebrews 12:1

Let us throw off everything that hinders and the sin that so easily entangles.

And let us run with perseverance the race marked out for us.

➔   **START** Real life with Jesus starts when you make the most enormous choice ever—trusting him to forgive your sins, make you right with God, and give you a forever home in heaven. Real life is also jam-packed with other choices both big and small☐ each presenting you with an opportunity to stick close to Jesus or to walk the other way. Moment by moment, only you can decide what to do.

Why not just flip out and make bad choices?

➔   **READ** Hebrews 12:1-3

> ¹Therefore, since we are surrounded by such a great cloud of witnesses, let us throw off everything that hinders and the sin that so easily entangles. And let us run with perseverance the race marked out for us, ²fixing our eyes on Jesus, the pioneer and perfecter of faith. For the joy set before him he endured the cross, scorning its shame, and sat down at the right hand of the throne of God. ³Consider him who endured such opposition from sinners, so that you will not grow weary and lose heart.

➔   **THINK** Just before that passage, the book of Hebrews presents its "Hall of Faith," a chapter full of people who followed their Lord faithfully. They're the "cloud of witnesses" in heaven who now "surround" us and watch us run the race of faith. It's like having your own cosmic cheering squad.

When you run a race, what might hinder or entangle you? Why get rid of those things?

The fastest runners in the world wear the lightest and most aerodynamic clothing possible. Ancient athletes sometimes ran naked, refusing to let anything slow them down. In this passage things that "hinder" aren't bad in themselves, but they thwart your all-out effort. Sins that "entangle," on the other hand, inevitably trip you up and send you sprawling. By the way, the race pictured here in Hebrews is no sprint. It's a long-distance race that can only be done with concentration and determination.

How did Jesus choose to see the cross—the incredibly painful thing that stood between him and the finish line?

What good could it possibly do to "fix your eyes on Jesus," thinking of him as your example? How does his struggle inspire you—or not?

➔   **LIVE** What good things in life—people, activities, attitudes—get in the way of your growing closer to God and making the very best choices? What sins keep tripping you up as you try to follow Jesus?

As you wrap up *Choose*, what's your plan to keep making amazingly great choices? Who's going to help you? What goals do you have for growth?

➔   **WRAP** Making good choices isn't just about deciding to do the right things. It's about seizing your chance to stick close to Jesus, to follow in his path, and to live tight with him always. He's not just the One who tells you to wise up and do good to others. He's your reason for every great choice you can ever make. Choose well.

» MORE THOUGHTS TO MULL

- What race does God have "marked out" for you?

- How badly do you want to excel in the race of following Jesus?

- Make sure you have a plan to keep getting closer to Jesus. Do the first step of your plan today.

» MORE SCRIPTURES TO DIG

- Open a Bible to Hebrews 12:1-3 and read what comes before and after it. **Hebrews 11** is that "Hall of Faith" that tells the story of countless believers who've gone before you, people whose lives can show you how to stay tight with God no matter what. **Hebrews 12:4-12** explains that God uses life's tough moments to discipline us to obey him, in the same way a strenuous workout routine gets us in peak physical condition. It says, "No discipline seems pleasant at the time, but painful. Later on, however, it produces a harvest of righteousness and peace for those who have been trained by it" (Hebrews 12:11). It goes on, "Therefore, strengthen your feeble arms and weak knees. 'Make level paths for your feet'" (Hebrews 12:12-13). God's training is what enables you to run hard and fast.

- Check this version of **Hebrews 12:3** (NCV) for an easy-to-remember encouragement to choose good: "Think about Jesus' example. He held on while wicked people were doing evil things to him. So do not get tired and stop trying."

- You might figure that Jesus had it easy when it came to doing the right thing. Think again. Just like you, he had to choose to go God's way. See what **Hebrews 5:7-8** has to say about that. One snippet: "Even though Jesus was the Son of God, he learned obedience by what he suffered" (Hebrews 5:8, NCV).

Many people think teenagers aren't capable of much. But Zach Hunter is proving those people wrong. He's only fifteen, but he's working to end slavery in the world—and he's making changes that affect millions of people. Find out how Zach is making a difference and how you can make changes in the things that you see wrong with our world.

Be the Change
Your Guide to Freeing Slaves and Changing the World
Zach Hunter
RETAIL $9.99
ISBN 0-310-27756-6

Visit www.invertbooks.com or your local bookstore.

Most teenagers think that being a Christian means doing the right thing, but figuring out what the "right thing" is can be a challenge. It's difficult for students to tell the difference between God's plan for them and what other Christians say is God's plan for them. Author Mark Matlock will guide your students through God's Word to help them figure out what God really wants from them.

What Does God Want from Me?
Understanding God's Desire for Your Life
Mark Matlock
RETAIL $9.99
ISBN 0-310-25815-4

If you've ever wondered if God is really there and listening, if you're good enough, or what's so great about heaven, you're not alone. We all have had personal questions, but the answers are often harder to come by. In this book, you'll discover how to navigate your big questions, and what the answers mean for your life and faith.

Living with Questions
Dale Fincher
RETAIL $9.99
ISBN 0-310-27664-0

Love This! contains real-life stories of people like you who've found ways to love their neighbors. It will challenge you to make a difference in your world by loving people who are often ignored or unloved—the homeless, the addicted, the elderly, those of different races, even your enemies—and show you tangible ways you can demonstrate that love.

Love This!
Learning to Make It a Way of Life, Not Just a Word
Andy Braner
RETAIL $12.99
ISBN 0-310-27380-3

Visit www.invertbooks.com or your local bookstore.